The Break-Up Book

How to Avoid, Leave, and Recover from Negative Relationships

ACE METAPHOR

D1510772

DEDICATION

To my mother, I love you.

To my father, I look up to you.

To my Metaphorically Speaking family, this wouldn't
have been possible without you.

To my online supporters, you give me purpose – for
that I am grateful.

Thank you for believing in me.

Connect with me on social media:

Facebook.com/acemetaphor

Instagram.com/acemetaphor

Send a picture of yourself holding the book to acemetaphorpoetry@gmail.com.

Be sure to include your social media handle.

Be creative, you may be featured on one of my social media pages.

Love to you all.

Table of Contents

Avoid 1

Pre-Relationship 2

Unapologetically Single 3

Repel 4

Chivalry 5

Pro-bae-tion Period 6

Floor Model 7

Geppetto 8

Times Two 9

Shipping and Handling 10

At My Worst 11

Wait for What 12

Let Me See Those Hands 13

Beware of Bored People 14

Step to Me Correct 15

WYD Culture 16

In Your Feelings 17

Go With the Flow 18

The We Are Just Friends Card 19

What He Said 20

Childish 21

Keep It 22

Not Worried about Me 23

Edges 24

Trying to Get You to Like Them 25

Convince Someone to Like You 26

Heightened Form 27

Value 28

A Future With You 29

Ring Worthy 30

This Guy vs. That Guy 31

Thermostat 32

Deck of Cards 33

Number 2 34

Hard Being Super 35

Playing Hard to Get 36

Are You in the Bed? 37

Legs for a Reason 38

Why I'm Single 39

Inheritance 40

Leave 41

Less Bullshitty 42

Ring Is not a Bandage 43

The Wrong Person 44

Imaginary Relationship 45

Closer to Perfection 46

Trustworthy Enough 47

Healthy Relationship 48

First Step to Rehab 49

Bigger than Somebody's Wife 50

Self-Love Muscle 51

Loves You But 52

What I Love You Means 53

Against the World 54

Love Is a Tool 55

Different Language 56

Work And 57

Elevate-her 58

Posting..59

Forgiveness Bank...60

Direct Questions..61

Uncertainty Words 62

Lie Is the Reason 63

Afraid of Honesty..64

Problems 65

Needs Are the Reason You Cheated.................................66

Love and Leave..67

Think vs. Know..68

Being...69

Placeholding..70

Walk Away...71

Okay Love 72

Sixty Days 73

Recover...74

Love Has Your Back..75

Heartbreak 76

Cleanse Your Palate 77

Your Soulmate?...78

8:01...79

Don't Subtract...80

Finger Button 81

Give-a-Fuck Budget..82

It takes Heart..83

We Isn't We..84

Capable...85

Representative..86

From Over There 87

Lonely in a Relationship 88

Leech. 89

Where Was This? 90

Need vs. Want 91

Prove Them Wrong 92

List for YOU 93

Sorry 94

Closure 95

Walk into Your Sunshine 96

Love What Makes Me, Me 97

What about You 98

Not to Heal 99

It's Your Job 100

Not Stressed 101

Smile Regardless 102

About Ace Metaphor 103

Avoid

Avoid negative relationships.

Pre-Relationship

Your next successful relationship starts…right now. It's the pre-relationship phase. The decisions you make right now in the comfort of your single space can and will affect your next relationship, maybe your last relationship.

Most long-lasting relationships sprouted forth from two persons who readied themselves long before they met.

Envision what type of spouse you want to be. Do you currently resemble her? Many people make the mistake of waiting until they find their mate to make adjustments, not realizing how much more difficult those changes will be while trying to grow a new relationship. Securing a job, finishing college or reworking personality flaws are much more easily done without the distraction of courting someone.

So use your time wisely now. View your single life as an extension of the marriage you will eventually enjoy. Think about it—this is the only time you can focus exclusively on you, growing you and loving you. Your future husband will be thankful that you did, that you took full advantage of the pre-relationship.

Remember, the success of your future relationship starts with the work you put in as a single person.

Unapologetically Single

Be single, unapologetically. Yes, self-centered, even. Do things that make you happy even if others don't understand. It's not your job to be less in love with yourself to make them more comfortable, so stop apologizing for living the life you want. This is what your singleness is for. Use it explore, learn and grow, unbound from the expectations of others that only weigh you down. Some will say, "That's why you're single," as if self-love is a bad thing. The right person for you, is you. Let them know you're not going to say sorry for recognizing that.

Remember, it's important to find what makes you happy before you concern yourself with what makes a man happy— even if people don't get it.

Repel

Right now, there's a woman out there who's running her own business, doing her thing, and enjoying a successful career. Maybe that person is you. And you have a great personality. But you're repelling people because your success intimidates the wrong type of men. Unfortunately, you've been questioning whether or not you should dim yourself so you can attract more men. Don't.

You have to realize that your strong and independent nature, your queendom, is your bullshit repellent. If people are insecure with themselves, they don't deserve you and your success.

Why are you trying to change who you are just to attract more men who are wrong for you anyway? The right person for you will see your success as a blessing. They'll see the fact that you are handling business as an asset, and they'll love you and cherish you even more. Quit trying to please more people who don't like you. Instead, worry about pleasing the people who do.

Remember, your success is your bullshit repellent.

Chivalry

Queens, unless otherwise directed by whatever the fuck you want to do, you accept applications! You are the dream "job" that everyone desires and wishes to obtain. You are the prize. You are the CEO of "any man would be lucky to have me" Incorporated.

As the boss of you, you set the standard that dating prospects must meet. This is no different from any other organization. Some jobs require degrees, experience, good credit, a clean background check and solid references. Why shouldn't the person that shows interest in being selected to fill the most important role in your life meet those same standards, if you desire them to?

Stop feeling sorry for people who don't have what it takes to live up to what you require. Denying applications for your heart is a hard but vital task all queens must do to protect, grow and sustain their investments.

Remember, only accept applications when you are ready to have the position filled. Name one job where people are interviewed for fun. I'll wait.

Pro-bae-tion Period

You're dating. The person passed the interview. They're showing signs of promise. So you're tempted to give them the full-time benefits package.

Before you do, consider this—most companies have a probationary period for new employees. It's an extended evaluation so you fully understand the new hire's merits, strengths and weaknesses. Shouldn't you do the same in your love life?

Dating is not the position you interview people for, right? Nor was boyfriend. Marriage was the job title, correct? So shouldn't marriage be the time where full-time benefits are given? Benefits like lifelong commitments, children, unconditional love and great personal sacrifices?

This would make anything prior to marriage, pro-bae-tion. Think of exclusive dating as this extended evaluation. It's the time you pay close attention to every move, action and word to see if they're worthy of your hand in marriage. Just like at a company, if the trial period is successful and there are no call-offs or write-ups, then it's time for marriage and all its benefits.

Remember, never be a wife to a boyfriend—they haven't earned it yet.

Floor Model

We think we're dating an actual person, but we're actually dating a floor model of the real thing.

A few weeks ago, I went to Ikea and bought a desk and two chairs. That's what I saw; I didn't pay for boxes, but they sent the products in boxes to my house. The instructions told me to put it together myself, but that's not what I paid for! They didn't have these boxes with instructions on the showroom floor. They didn't tell customers like me, "Buy these boxes, and put together these products." They're misleading people.

In dating, the same things can happen. A person shows up in your life and says, "Hold on. This dating persona isn't actually me. That was my floor model self. That's my potential. If you put in the work and assemble me, you can teach me how to be the person I need to be."

Whoa...what? Shouldn't you have been using the last thirty years of your life to do that? You waited all this time for me to build you? No. Find me after you assemble yourself. The only thing we should have to work on in this relationship is the relationship itself! Not personal issues we should have addressed long before we met. Find the closure you need first. Mend that broken heart you're carrying first. Fix yourself before you come to my house. That's your responsibility, not mine.

Remember, soul mates come with no assembly required.

Geppetto

Thinking you can change somebody is the fastest way to get hurt.

Unless your name is Geppetto, you have no business trying to build a bae or build a boo. But that's often what we try to do. We tell ourselves we can fix someone. "I can make them a real man or a real woman. Let me put my stuffing inside that person. Here's a splash of faithfulness, a pinch of morals, some handsomeness, and some new clothes. Now come to life, come to life!"

That's the problem; we think we can mold another person into the likeness we desire, instead of finding what we need in a person that already possesses those qualities. Life is no fairy tale. Thinking that we have the power to change ordinary boys and girls into real men or women with real marriage qualities is often how you get hurt. Despite our best effort, it is up to that individual whether or not they want to grow, learn or heal. Unless you can find that magic pixie dust.

Remember, if you think you can change another person, check your nose right now, Pinocchio. Because you're lying to yourself.

Times Two

As a woman, your chromosomes have been gifted with a special power—a multiplication factor. When men bring you something, you can double it! He brings you himself, you make another—a baby. He has grind, you give him a reason to grind harder. You double his ambition!

But just as in math, your powers have limitations. When you multiply zero by any value, all you have is zero. Likewise, it's imperative that your man already possesses value that you can double. If a man starts with zero goals, zero skills, and zero motivation, no matter how great you are, multiplying your power by his zero leaves you both with nothing. So use your power as a woman wisely.

Remember, never try to multiply your something by his nothing.

Shipping and Handling

Love is free, but there are shipping and handling fees associated with said love. How are you going to love somebody when you can't even transport your half of the love to the date? You don't have a phone. You haven't paid your bills. You're in between jobs. Why date if you're not financially ready to contribute to a relationship?

Again, love is free, but the walls and roof that will cover the love and the children it creates is not. Yes, regardless of financial situations, everyone deserves to feel loved.

My rule of pinky is that you should at least have a place to constantly wash your ass before trying to court someone else. In Maslow's Hierarchy of Needs, a place to stay comes before finding a bae.

Remember, get your life in order before you step into someone else's.

At My Worst

When someone approaches you, they should be ready for you. This whole "if you don't want me at my worst, you don't deserve me at my best" thing is so misused nowadays.

I get it, a person may be down on their luck or in between jobs. They might be going through some type of hardship stemming from conditions that may or may not have been under their control. But there is a time and a place for everything, and a person's worst is not the time for them to date or court another person. The fact that they're dating when they should be getting their lives together is more of a concern than the actual problems they're going through.

Priorities, people. Expect people to be disciplined enough to only date at their best, for that tells you they understand the importance of taking care of their responsibilities first. How can a person live up to other people's expectations for them as a mate when they don't even live up to the expectations they have for themselves?

Remember, if that person isn't at their best, they shouldn't blame others for not wanting to get into a relationship with them.

Wait for What?

Some people like you but don't have what it takes to take your relationship to the next level—a place of commitment. So what do they do? They give you something to hold on to like a title. Girlfriend, boo, or whatever just to buy more time to get ready or to stall. These titles offer no real security or promises. They're a string. Far too often, we jump at the chance to hold on to that string.

"Girl, I'm his girlfriend. I'll do anything for my man."

Shouldn't that be, "You'll do anything for your husband"?

Too often we allow empty titles to drag us into fruitless relationships for far too long. Yes, those terms of supposed endearment keep us from walking away from a relationship that proves over time to get us no closer to the real goal—marriage.

Granted, we should expect people to have genuine intentions and fulfill promises, but think about it. When do you say, "For better or for worse, through sickness and in health, 'til death do us part"? When agreeing to be someone's girlfriend? You don't say that! There are no real promises when you date. Until those words are uttered at an altar, keep control of your future. Avoid being tied down by meaningless titles.

Remember, you can't get strung along if you never take ahold of the string.

Let Me See Those Hands

Sometimes you have to grab somebody by the wrist and say, "Let me see those hands. I'm just making sure you're strong enough to handle what you asked for from me."

Guess what—I'm pretty strong. I'm independent. People say they want that from a person before they're sure they can handle it. I've been hurt too many times that way. So I've learned to inspect the hands of even the best intentioned potential suitors to see if they have what it takes.

Carrying the burden of being with the type of awesome person I am can be a task, and I've put too much work into becoming a complete package to be dropped by a weak-handed person. I value my self-esteem, self-confidence and self-love too much for them to be broken by another person.

For you, it's important to know if the person you're dating is jealous or insecure. Even people who say they want a strong person bring out the worst of themselves when someone exercises their independent nature.

Remember, check those hands every time.

Beware of Bored People

Bored people. Bored people. Bored people.

Beware of people who have nothing else better to do. They'll play with people's hearts just for entertainment. They'll date not with intentions, but to get out of the house. They'll call not to grow a relationship, but to pass time.

We have to safeguard against our hearts becoming someone else's play thing. A heart is too valuable to end up in the hands of a person like that. It's important for us to know how to identify these kinds of daters.

One way is to ask yourself, does this person make plans far in advance with you, or text you randomly at the last minute wanting to hang, but with no real date ideas? People who date you with clear intentions do so with forethought, while people who don't only think of you on a night when boredom strikes.

Remember, you deserve more than the latter. You should expect to be more than just some guy's entertainment.

Step to Me Correct

Do you ever look at somebody when they try to step to you the wrong way?

You're like, "Who the hell do you think you are?"

Then you tell them you aren't even mad because of the way they're stepping to you. "Yo, why don't you come through? Why don't you come through?"

For a second, you find yourself getting mad at them. But then you tell yourself not to be. Instead, you're going to get mad at all those other people, all those other girls or all those other men who made you think that was okay.

In this world, there are people who are willing to take "good enough."

"Yeah, he's alright. He has a job. He doesn't have too many felonies. That makes for successful relationship material."

Really? You're blowing my mind. Just because that little stuff you do works on this other person or that other person doesn't mean it's going to work on an extraordinarily deserving person like me. You have to step correct—or don't step at all. I know what I deserve.

Remember, it's not what people try to give you, it's what you're willing to accept.

WYD Culture

The "WYD" culture is killing love. It's strangling chivalry. It's destroying romance.

We need to bring the "I'm coming over at 8:00; made reservations at your favorite restaurant two weeks ago; gave you three days' notice so you can make plans; I'm going to pick you up; bring you flowers and knock on your door; and when you open up the door, your favorite jazz band is going to be playing," culture back.

That's the culture that breeds love. It's wonderful when you know a man put in thought and effort to win your attention!

Require men to court you like our parents did. If a man expects you to open up your plans for him, to sacrifice time with your family, goals, school, and job to be with him, he should step to you correct. No random texts at 11:00 p.m. are worth that. So stop that "WYD" nonsense, or you'll kill off your own chance at finding love.

Remember, "WYD" never leads to "I love you."

In Your Feelings

Let's pretend your feelings are streets. Be careful who you cross the street for.

Sometimes, we step out into the middle of the road, right in the middle of feelings for a person, then get hit by the bullshit they send our way.

They be like, "Come here! Come here! I'm a good guy! I'm a good girl! I'm going to treat you well! I'm going to always have your back!" or, "I am not going to lie to you. I swear I'm telling the truth."

Then what do you say?

"Oh, that sounds good. Here I come, okay!"

We eagerly leave the safety of the sidewalk of singleness without looking both ways, before stepping foot into the vulnerability of relationships.

Get to know who they are first. Do they seem to be trustworthy, and do they have pure intentions? Are they careful? A careful person will make sure the coast is clear, free of unnecessary pitfalls and dangers before asking you to cross the street for them.

Properly vet any potential dating partner and the life they're inviting you into so you don't get blindsided.

Remember, always look both ways before crossing into a relationship.

Go With the Flow

Have you ever spoken to someone for an extended period of time, and thought about investing in a relationship with them? Putting in more time, energy, effort, and attention?

You ask them a simple question like, "Hey man, where do you see this relationship going?" And they hit you with one of these, "Tsk. Man, can't you just go with the flow?"

If you say to me, I have to fall back, and you don't know how I fit into your life, then I'm not going to invest my time, energy, and effort into winning you.

Today, the worst relationship heartbreakers are no longer thugs, drug dealers, or alcoholics. They're the people who don't know what they want in life. Yet they hold onto us while they try to figure it out. Then when they figure out that we aren't it, they break our hearts and let us go. So no, I can't go with the flow.

Remember, sometimes happiness is upstream.

The "We Are Just Friends" Card

It's important in all relationships to define things. Establishing an understanding helps manage expectations and ensure that both parties are on the same page and that they're travelling in a similar direction. But at times, we enjoy the ride of a relationship so much that we forget to ask where we're going or what the journey means for our lives together and as individuals.

You may have assumed you two were heading to Commitment Lane, but he's thinking you two are going to Just-a-Friend Avenue. Don't wait until you've reached that undesirable destination to start asking the questions you should've asked before you got ins his car.

"Where do you see this going?"

Remember, give yourself the option to decide if you want to go with him to where he plans to go.

What He Said

He said he isn't trying to have a relationship with you. What do you think that means? He said he wants to take it slow. What do you think that means?

He means exactly what he said! Stop trying to analyze what people tell you. When somebody says they like you but they don't want to be with you, that doesn't mean they like you but secretly want to be with you, so you just have to try harder. No, they mean exactly what they said.

Quit reading into sentences what's not there. Take people at face value. I get it, we may want them to love us, so we pretend to hear it. We want them to be with us, so we make excuses from their dismissive actions. It's going to be hard, but accepting the truth always is. You have to allow people to take responsibility for their words and assign credibility to them. Let their actual words influence your choices. Don't add unsaid meaning!

Remember, if a person really wants to be with you, they will *not* say that they don't. If they're lying about it, then you deserve better anyway.

Childish

Children put aside a toy, only to pick it up once again when they see another child playing with it. That's childish behavior. Unfortunately, some people never grow out of it. That's why, when you're trying to give somebody attention when you're single, they don't want you. It's not until somebody else picks you up and starts to play with you, giving you attention and treating you right, that they want you.

Childish people need other people to see your value before they do. But you deserve a grown man, a grown woman. Grown people will appreciate you and see your worth, even if somebody else doesn't see it first. They'll be glad they discovered you before somebody else did. That means they can take a hold of your heart. They can treat you right. They can grow with you. They can claim you. They can love you.

Remember, the right person for you doesn't need somebody else to love you first.

Keep It

What happens after he woos you? Makes you weak in the knees and sweeps you off your feet? Does he have a plan? Most men put thought into getting your attention, but very few put in any effort once they have it.

Dating should never stop the pursuit. Marriage isn't even the end goal—forever is. Unfortunately, some never understand this, so it's up to you to find out who does and who doesn't. Yes, it's awesome that someone sends you flowers, but is this just an attempt to win you over, or is thoughtfulness part of his personality? Distinguishing between the two is the difference between a lifetime of dating and a marriage devoid of romance.

Remember, you're not a prize to be won, then placed on a shelf to be forgotten.

Not Worried about Me

I'm at a point in life where I can't be worried about people whose actions prove they're not worried about me. I can't give you any more of my attention. I'm sorry, I'm too grown. I'm at the you-have-to-meet-me-halfway point in my life. That means I'm going to show you I'm interested, but I'm not going to chase you.

If somebody wants to be with you, they're going to show you that. They're going to reciprocate interest. They're not going to make you jump through hoops and over obstacles just to get to their heart. Those people aren't worried about you, they're worried about themselves.

You are the prize. They are too, so there should be reciprocity, not games of cat and mouse.

Remember, never go out of your way for people who are unwilling to meet you at least halfway there.

Edges

Does it feel like you're running in a hamster wheel? Are you chasing a person who doesn't want to get caught?

You're running and running after a guy, sweating out your edges and all, hoping he'll see your effort and reciprocate your love. You know the feeling: your hair grease is dripping all over your face, your asthma is kicking in, and you look around and realize you aren't getting anywhere.

Sometimes, no matter what you do, other people will not see your value and beauty, and it hurts. But you cannot let the hurt of rejection motivate you to keep trying and trying. I know your pride; your ego can't accept that the person you like doesn't like you back. But you'll lose valuable time on someone who doesn't value you when you could be with someone who does.

Remember, don't let good guys pass you by because you're chasing the wrong guy.

Trying to Get You to Like Them

Does that person really like you, or are you just trying to get them to like you?

Certain people play keep-away with their hearts. We fall for the game. We jump after their hearts because they put it just close enough for us to reach for it. We feel like we can finally grasp it, like the effort, energy, and time we've invested is finally going to pay off.

Then they yank it away and make us jump for it again. But it's only when we're on the brink of giving up, walking away, and finding our self-confidence again that they dangle their hearts in front of us one more time.

Why do people do that? Because they like it when we stroke their egos. People who want to be caught don't run away. People who are serious don't play games.

Remember, there is no way to stop others from playing keep-away with their hearts, but at least you can refuse to keep falling for the trick.

Convince Someone to Like You

I would beg you to stay. I would hit your phone up over and over and over again even though you don't answer. I would give you all of the reasons why I'm the perfect person for you.

But I just love myself a little too much to do that. I love myself a little too much to convince somebody to see the value in me that they should see for themselves. I just can't do it. My self-esteem is too valuable. I can't let you crush it. My self-esteem is my main ingredient for me being successful in a future relationship, and if you're proving to me that you don't want me, I can't sacrifice how I feel about myself for you. I'm not going to let you damage me for another person. So no, if you don't want to stay, leave. I choose me every time.

Remember, never convince someone to like you.

Heightened Form

You really like that person, and you want so badly for them to like you back so much so that you are willing to do anything it takes to attract them. Even if that means changing who you are, what you like, and the company you keep. You become a pretender. One that looks in the mirror and barely recognizes yourself. All for what? For someone who couldn't see or appreciate the beautiful person you were all along? At times, we are tempted to lose who we are to find the wrong person's heart. But they'll only love you as long as you continue to be someone you're not. You will never be able to keep up that façade, that form, that illusion.

You can be you every day for the rest of your life, but you will never *be* somebody else for the rest of your life. That's how you end up losing two hearts.

Remember, if you have to pretend in a relationship, then that person isn't right for you.

Value

Life is chess, not checkers. You should never accept being just another piece on the board of someone's life. You are a queen, right? Shouldn't you be treated and valued as such?

To a man, a capable queen makes moves for him that no other piece can. Refuse to allow any man to take your versatility for granted as if you're commonplace. Name another person in his life that can be his nurse when he gets sick or his therapist when problems arise or his best friend who gives him children. I'll save you time—no one can. Don't allow what you add to his life to be devalued. Don't accept pawn-like treatment. You are not disposable.

Remember, protect the sacredness of your crown by yoking yourself only to a king who appreciates you.

A Future With You

Every man who approaches you and shows interest does it for a similar reason—the future. Yes, every man sees some way that you fit into his future, and it's your job to decipher what kind of future that is.

Is it the kind of future you deserve? "Future wife" sounds very fitting, but is that what he's offering? Sadly, many suitors today try to fit you into a future that's convenient for them, short-lived and unbecoming of your queendom.

How does "future baby mom" sound to you? Or "future side piece"? What about "future live-in girlfriend"? I'm sure these aren't the futures you dreamed about as a child.

It's important for you to figure out as quickly as possible what future a man is asking of you. Understand, this is no easy task for many reasons, some of which include dishonestly, deception, or, frankly, utter uncertainty on their part. Don't be patient with people who don't see a long-term future with you. They deserve short-term patience.

Remember, just because a man sees a future with you doesn't mean you have to see one with him, especially if you're envisioning two different futures.

Ring Worthy

I was once asked by a young lady, "Ace, how do you know if I'm ring worthy?"

"Ring worthy to whom?" I asked her back.

She said, "To the right man."

That broke my heart. She thinks somebody else has the right to determine her worth as a woman! A man has no right to dictate to you what you deserve or what qualities you should bring to the table. You determine those things. You decide if you are marriage material or not.

"Ring worthy"? That should never be how you evaluate yourself. Like your many complexities can be summed up in a gold band!

You don't need anyone's permission to know you're special. Stop waiting on it. If you want a ring, go buy one. You don't need anyone to give it to you.

Remember, you're ring worthy whether a man says so or not.

This Guy vs. That Guy

You can be in a relationship with a guy and think something is wrong with you. You might be like, "Damn, can I be submissive? Can I follow somebody's lead?"

You start questioning yourself because you're with *this* guy and not *that* guy.

That guy doesn't have to say, "Respect me." If a guy has to say, "You will respect me," he isn't *that* guy. He's *this* guy. This guy ought to say please a little bit more.

That guy commands respect by the way he carries himself, the love he shows, and the trust he earns, but this guy thinks that being born a man gives him the right to lead. It's hard for any woman to follow a guy like that.

Regardless of what man you meet, it is important to work on becoming the type of wife you want to be. No person can bring something out of you that you don't already possess.

Remember, always question the guy you're with—is he *this* guy or *that* guy?

Thermostat

You invite somebody over to your home, walk into the hallway, and see that person adjusting your thermostat. They say, "Man, it's a little hot in here. I'm just going to turn on the cold air."

"Whoa, don't you touch my thermostat! Hold on!"

When is the last time you let somebody touch your thermostat? Yes, the one you're paying the energy bill for! Never.

Yet we invite people into our lives and let them adjust the thermostat of our hearts to suit them, not us. They don't live here, and there's no ring on their finger! So why do you keep letting the guest in the home of your heart change the conditions of it to make themselves more comfortable?

If we let people come in, turn on the air conditioner, and leave, we'll be left with the bill! So set your thermostat to what you want, and other people can live with it or not.

Remember, people at best are just leasing space in our lives.

Deck of Cards

Finding your soulmate sometimes feels like randomly going through a deck of cards. You know there are fifty-two cards and, odds are, you're going to get a face value card at some point. But sometimes, you have to go through a lot of fours and sixes and nines before you find your king.

Don't get discouraged. I know you've flipped over a two, a four, a five, a six, and a seven. You keep getting low value cards, those low value men and women. But there are still four kings in the deck of life.

The problem isn't that you keep drawing low value men from the dating pool, it's that you keep placing those men in your hand instead of immediately discarding them so you can redraw and try another. The quicker you can discard, the quicker you get another chance.

Remember, your king is in that deck. You just have to quickly throw away the jokers to find him.

Number 2

I am absolutely okay with being second in someone's life. I don't mean the second place where you leave me for someone else. I'm referring to you as your first place and me as your second. I want *you* to be your number one, your first priority. I want you to always take care of yourself, to value yourself, to respect yourself.

My role in this relationship is not to get you to treat me better than you treat yourself, it's to love the person you are. I understand that when you put yourself first, it directly benefits me. What makes you happy makes me happy, and I never want you to change that. So I'm okay with being number two as long as you're number one.

Remember, second place still wins a medal.

Hard Being Super

Being superhuman sounds really appealing until you look to your left and your right. Then you realize there aren't a lot of people flying around this earth like you. Not many people use phone booths to change into their costumes. You haven't met another person with an "S" on their chest.

You're being Superwoman or Superman in your own life, but maybe you're not supposed to find somebody with those same powers. Maybe you're supposed to find somebody who makes you feel special inside, makes you feel loved inside. Maybe they're able to reciprocate that feeling.

Lois Lane can't fly, but Superman loved her. She was the one person he wanted to live for above everything else.

Yes, you've got super powers, and you're awesome. But life feels lonely because there isn't another person who can relate. So maybe it's somebody down on earth who will love you and make you feel special inside, and that's all the relationship you will need.

Remember, not all superheroes fly. Some just love you the way you are.

Playing Hard to Get

You should have high standards. Those elevated expectations protect you from subpar treatment and attention. Keep in mind that someone who wants your heart will earn it. You deserve to be earned—*earned*, not chased. Many refer to the Good Book by saying, "He who finds a wife finds a good thing."

True. But note the word "find," not "chase." Finding implies that you've identified what's missing in your life. You've searched high and low to discover it.

If something is going to be found, it's going to be stationary. That's how it gets located in the first place.

Are you stationary? Are you staying busy doing things that good people do while taking care of yourself? That's where good men look to find a mate.

Or are you running away from them, expecting the right man to run after you? Are you spending more time playing hard to get than working hard on getting your life together?

Remember, when he comes into your life, you will not have to play games. All you will have to do is continue being you, for you are exactly who he has been looking for this whole time.

Are You in the Bed?

There you go again in that bed, scrolling on social media and watching Netflix. It's the weekend!

This is probably, what, your fourth weekend in a row doing that? I hope you never ask, "Where are all the good men at?" because my very sarcastic reply, "Probably right outside," will undoubtedly irritate you. But isn't that the truth?

We expect our soulmate to be delivered to our doorstep as if they could be ordered from Amazon. Sorry, sis. Your Prime account provides no benefits here.

The real question is, are you ready to date with the intention of being married? Some people date for fun, pleasure, or entertainment. If those are the goals, I'd rather be barricaded in the house as well. It's a lot safer. Plus, I'm anti-social.

But if we're eagerly seeking a mate to marry, that's worth logging out of Hulu for the night and grabbing a drink or saying yes to co-workers' attempts to get you to join them for an outing.

Your soulmate is probably somewhere just out of reach from your comfort zone, especially if that comfort zone is your bedroom on a Friday night. It's hard enough to find a remote while you're in the bed, so I know it's almost impossible to find a husband that way.

Remember, there is always eHarmony if going out doesn't work out. There are many means to a happy ending.

Legs for a Reason

You've been given two legs for a reason. They're to be used for your life journey on the path you're destined to walk. No one can walk it for you, nor can you for them.

Along the way to your happiness, you may meet a man heading to the same place you are. You may agree to travel together. Down the road—the same road—you may decide to become partners and get married. In doing so, you agree to help each other navigate any obstacles standing in the way of your two individual journeys that you're now walking together.

Notice—he will not try to walk for you, he will walk for himself, and you will not try to guide him, for his path was already set before he met you. You two will continue to walk, using your own legs, down the same road you both agreed to walk on long before finding each other. That's what love is.

Remember, your walk is your own.

Why I'm Single

People ask me why I'm single. It makes me lose my mind.

"I don't know. Why don't you ask all the people who don't want me back?"

For a relationship to work, somebody has to agree to be in a relationship with me. It takes two, you know. I can't force somebody to be with me.

Right now, I'm just in between the people who want me back. There's nothing wrong with me. In fact, there's nothing wrong with any person just because they're single. They just haven't found the person who wants them back. Sometimes they're soulmates, sometimes they're not.

I'm waiting for somebody who will think, "Damn. I can't believe somebody slept on you. I can't believe they didn't see what I see in you. I'm so happy to have you in my life. Where would I be without you?"

I'm waiting for the person who agrees to be with me because they want to be with me. That's why I'm single.

Remember, being single doesn't mean you're broken.

Inheritance

If you have ten dollars in your bank account today but know that your direct deposit hits at midnight, you're stressing too much. You're about to be balling in a matter of hours.

Now imagine you have a trust fund you can access in a matter of months. Are you tripping about the amount of money you have in your hand right now? No.

So why would we allow ourselves to be lonely in the present when we know that, just around the corner, our partner is coming?

He's your inheritance. You do believe he's coming, right? If not, *start*. Not believing he's on his way makes you dwell on the ten dollars you have instead of the direct deposit that's sure to come.

Just as we can become poor in mind, we can become lonely in spirit, only giving attention to our present single state and ignoring the blessing that's sure to come our way in due season.

A blinded state of mind can affect the choices we make. We can become desperate and settle for anything to satisfy our needs. I know it's hard, but relax. There's plenty of time left—so make every decision knowing that you are the future wife of the right person for you.

Remember, it's not a matter of *if*, but *when*.

There are people in this life who will build you up and those who will tear you down. Which type of person do you want to spend the rest of your life with? Let me tell you the truth—if that person asking you out doesn't treat you like a queen, they don't deserve to be your king, ever.

Avoid negative relationships.

Leave

Leave that negative relationship.

Less Bullshitty

Committing to a bullshit relationship won't make it less bullshitty. You think saying, "I do," is going to make it smell like roses? You think having somebody's child is going to make him stay with you? You think moving in with him is going to make your problems go away?

What you were before you decided to commit is what you are afterwards. As a matter of fact, commitment multiplies it by fifty. Think about it—you've been with this person a year, and all you've had are problems, tears, and arguments. You think fifty more years is going to change anything?

Your first year with somebody was supposed to be the best year of your lives. There shouldn't have been major problems. They shouldn't have been comfortable enough with you to yell at you, disrespect you, or cheat on you, but they did.

So what do you think is going to happen when you commit deeper in that relationship? Multiply that first year by fifty. How do you feel about that?

Remember, just because you commit doesn't mean things are going to change. You're just going to get more of the same.

Ring Is Not a Bandage

When somebody gives you a ring, hopefully it means they love you, that they're ready to spend a fruitful life together with you, that they're already committed in their heart, that they just want a ring to be the outward expression of their determination to spend life with you.

When somebody gives you a ring, it says, "I love you," not, "I'm sorry." It's not a bandaid. A ring is not a way to fix your shortcomings or your problems. Just because you give somebody a ring doesn't mean they're going to be forced to work.

People think, "Well, this ring is going to change our relationship, 'cause now we've got to work through something." Just because you want to work through it doesn't mean you will. Maybe he doesn't know how. Maybe you don't either.

When somebody gives you a ring, it should be because they're ready to spend the rest of their life with you, not because they're ready to apologize for taking your relationship for granted. A ring should not draw you closer to them for the wrong reasons. Marriage is perfect, but sometimes, we use it imperfectly. Don't let somebody use a ring like that with you.

Remember, a ring is not a bandaid.

The Wrong Person

If you had been patient and disciplined enough, if you knew yourself enough to know what you needed, what you didn't, what made you better, and what made you worse, you wouldn't have to change that person you're with right now because you would've picked the right person.

Sometimes, we get in relationships with the wrong people, and we over-compensate for our initial wrong decision with lust-fueled actions, short-term thinking, and void-filling behaviors. We should've filled those voids ourselves. But it's too late now, so we overcompensate by trying to change them. Not because we want to see them be better for them, but because we want them to be the right person for us! We simply can't accept the fact that we chose the wrong person.

This is a dangerous cycle. You'll never be able to change the wrong guy into the one you should've waited for in the first place. So while you're single now, take your time. This is not a race.

Remember, it's so much easier to stay out of wrong relationships than it is to get out of them.

Imaginary Relationship

If you can't touch, see, hear, smell, and taste the qualities, ideals, and goals of the person you're in a relationship with, then you're currently in a relationship with *something*, not someone. That something is yet-to-exist potential.

Potential will make you say, "Girl, I know he treats me bad, he has a temper, and he's between jobs, but he's going to be successful. He's going to be this. He's going to be that. That's why I like him."

He may never turn into that person. It's unfair to you and to him to care more about his potential than the real person he is now. There are way too many people in imaginary relationships who are completely oblivious to this. It's important to value the realness of now and keep the value of potential in its proper place.

Remember, potential won't pay bills or warm hearts.

Closer to Perfection

"No one is perfect."

People justify toxic relationships by relying on this adage. While that is true, some people are closer than others to being perfect for *you*.

The person you're with now may be a control freak, prone to jealousy, or narcissistic. Avoid being baited into staying with, "Nobody's perfect." You're the one who has to deal with that person's imperfections.

No one should put their hands on you. No one should cheat on you, justifying their actions by saying that's what men (or women) do.

There are people out there who can control themselves. They may not be perfect, but they won't hurt you.

Remember, no one is perfect, but someone *can* be perfect for you.

Trustworthy Enough

No matter how many times you unlock your phone for them to go through. No matter how many times you tell them who you're with or where you're going. No matter how many times you lose your dignity because they treat you like you're not husband or wife material.

You will never be trustworthy enough for an insecure person. They will always try to dig more and more and more out of you.

You're a grown person, but it feels like you're in a relationship with your Mom or your Dad. They need you to feed their jealousy, their possessiveness, their low self-esteem. No matter how much you may try to, it will never be enough. You have to be able to say, "You can't trust me, so you don't need to be with me."

If you've done everything you could within reason to prove that you're trustworthy but they still can't trust you, you have to separate.

Remember, nobody should feel like they aren't loveable or trustworthy when they are.

Healthy Relationship

We have to remove ourselves from unhealthy relationships before we normalize them. It's not okay to continue being subjected to bad words and belittlement. It's not okay to be consistently controlled and mentally abused. It's not healthy to be in a relationship that makes you cry more than smile. Those are not evidence of love.

But we ignore the warning signs. We refuse to break the cycle and allow our mental walls to be penetrated. We stay long enough for that person's unhealthy, jealous tendencies to seem normal. Yes, ordinary, predictable, expected. No longer are we shocked or disappointed. Some people even start to confuse abusive traits with love.

"I know the only reason he yells at me is because he cares so much."

No, he has a temper problem. Stop making excuses. Stop accepting this treatment as a normal way of life. It isn't. Healthy relationships display love without control. It's my belief that love can only grow in an environment where partners allow each other to choose to love, not force them to love.

Remember, protect your power of choice at all costs. Let no one make you love them.

First Step to Rehab

So you're in a relationship with that toxic person. It's hurting you. Despite this conclusion and your many attempts to leave, quit, or heal yourself physically and mentally, you can't seem to kick the habit. That toxic person has a hold on you that you can't quite explain. Why?

Must be love that keeps you there, right? Or is it possible that an addiction to him and his negative habits might explain it better? Have you become so dependent on the dysfunction that you're crippled by it? Is his "love" the substance that gets you high from time to time, but the rest of the time destroys you from the inside? If so, he is not your love, he is your drug!

People get addicted to drugs for many reasons. Maybe yours started as an experiment. You gave him a chance despite the warnings from others because he made you feel so good. But then his love began to take you away from things you cared about the most, made you turn your back on friends, or maybe even influenced you to sacrifice dreams. Although you now see those harmful effects on your life, you can't leave because your body needs his love. Your body secretly longs for it. You hate how it feels when you try to leave—the withdrawal, the shakes setting in from loneliness. So you don't even try to quit him anymore.

That's not love, that's addiction, and it's one of the hardest things you will ever have to walk away from.

But you can! The first step to recovery is admitting you have an addiction.

So right now, accept that it is not love—that toxic person is a drug. Say it aloud, and let the healing began.

Remember to say no to drugs.

Bigger than Somebody's Wife

Are you giving up your dreams, hopes, and ambitions for a man? Are you sacrificing your direction in life? Are you letting go of your money, time, and energy just to get a man to like you?

We're not that special. Really. Fellas are simple. I don't understand why you would quit being who you are just to convince us to like you. You serve a bigger purpose than that. You've got dreams, hopes, and ambitions that are bigger than one man. So quit giving them up just for us fellas. The man who is going to really love you will embrace who you are as a whole person, as more than just his wife.

Remember, there's more to your life than being somebody's wife.

Self-Love Muscle

At times, we're with people who love us so good that we accidently stop doing the thing we did to fall in love with ourselves before we met them.

Do you remember the moment you fell in love with yourself? Was it on a date you took yourself out on? Was it after years of mediation and getting to yourself? Was it after all the compliments you gave yourself?

Those acts made your love muscle strong! Those dates, treats, and personal attention were how you exercised that muscle. But what happens when we get in a great relationship? We don't take ourselves on dates anymore because the other person does. We stop spending personal time with ourselves because they do. We no longer give ourselves compliments because they shower us with "enough." We stop using our self-love muscle, and it becomes weak even while the love in our relationship grows.

So continue to strengthen that muscle even after you get into a relationship. You never know when someone might take their love away and you need that self-love to make it through.

Remember, no one can love you enough for you.

Loves You But

It's simple—find someone who "loves you and," not someone who "loves you but." That's the secret to relationship success.

We all know that love is the foundation, but what are we building on love's name? Is the structure one that adds the "and's" that love needs to flourish?

For example, does he love you and care about you, love you and value you, love you and do the little things? Or is your love structure filled with "but's"? He loves you but he cheats, he loves you but he hurts you, he loves you but he doesn't know how to show it.

The quickest way to find out what kind of love you have is to look at how you describe your love structure to your friends, family and, most importantly, yourself. Do you say more "and's" or "but's" when referring to your relationship? Yes, the fact that he loves you is a given—but whether he loves you with "and" or "but" is what will determine the fate of the relationship.

Remember, love by itself will never be enough.

What I Love You Means

When somebody says, "I love you," guess what that means.

It means, "I love you."

It means, "I'm affectionate toward you."

It means, "I value you."

It means, "I appreciate you."

It means, "I'm going to hold you. I'm going to take care of you. I'm going to look after you because of the place you hold in my life."

It means, "My actions are going to back up my words."

It means, simply, "I love you."

Guess what "I love you," doesn't mean.

It doesn't mean, "I can treat you any way I want to, and you're going to be there for me because you love me."

It doesn't mean, "I can disrespect you."

It doesn't mean, "I can get comfortable."

It doesn't mean, "I can stop doing things that influenced you to love me in the first place."

If people confuse these with, "I love you," they don't understand the English language.

Remember, "I love you," means different things to different people. Be sure that whoever says it to you means it the exact way you do.

Against the World

It's me and you against the world, not each other—I will not fight against you. Don't confuse me being a fighter *for* this relationship with fighting *in* this relationship. No, there are too many outside forces to defend against to come home with my guard up.

When we become partners, we're teammates. We have a common goal—happiness.

What happened to that? Yes, disagreements arise, but we shouldn't be forced to fight each other to solve them. What happened to talking things out? What happened to us feeling like we're on the same side? I'm unhappy when we point fingers at each other. I'm unhappy having to watch my back inside my own home. I want to love you, but not like this. Let's go back to the days when the only fights we had were when we stood by each other's sides, conquering a common opponent. In those days, we held hands and watched problems fall—together. I miss those days. If I can't have those back again, we may have to reconsider this partnership.

Remember, your biggest fights should not take place in the house you call a home.

Love Is a Tool

Love is a powerful tool when wielded by a person who has mastered it. In the right hands, love can be used to build beautiful bonds and create magical moments that last lifetimes. But this same tool, in the wrong hands, can be devastating, tearing apart very promising connections.

Just because someone loves you doesn't mean they know how to successfully use that tool. Love without the skills needed to employ it correctly benefits no one. It's dangerous to any relationship.

Would you be comfortable using a jackhammer at your job? No, you haven't been trained. The tool would likely harm you and anyone around.

You don't operate a tool you have no expertise with, so why allow someone to use love with you if they haven't been educated on how to use it?

This is why we get hurt in relationships—we let our hearts get worked on by people who don't have skills to use love safely.

Remember, love is a tool. Is that person qualified to use it?

Different Language

You ever try to start a conversation with somebody who doesn't speak your language?

"Hey, how are you doing?"

"*¿Cómo estas tú?*"

"Huh?"

They speak Spanish, you speak English. You can't communicate because you don't share a language. That doesn't mean the person can't express how they feel, they just don't know how to express it in a way you understand.

Sometimes, people get in a relationship but realize they love in two different languages. They love differently. They vibe differently. They give differently. When it comes to love, to actions, to words, one speaks Spanish and one speaks English. It's not wrong, it's just different.

Find somebody who speaks love like you do. Don't say hello to someone who says hola.

Remember, love is a language like any other.

Work And

He wants you to work and come home and do the dishes. Work and clean. Work and cook. Work and raise his kids. Work and hit the gym, keep that body sexy, and dress nice. Work and still be thoughtful and interested in his life. Work and then come and be his porn star.

He wants you to work and be a lady, a woman, and wife while he works and sits his ass on the couch.

That isn't how this works. He can't just go to work and think that's the end of his contributions to this relationship thing. It's a partnership. If he wants a woman who works and does all those things, tell him he has to be a husband who works and does those same things he asks of you. Tell him to cook and clean, too. Tell him he needs to raise his kids, too. Tell him to be a porn star, too.

Remember, a man has be willing to give what he wants to receive.

Elevate-her

Do you have an elevate-her? A man who helps you rise in life as if you two were on an elevator?

When you're with the right person, you both ascend together toward happiness, to a lifetime of laughs and smiles. One works so the other can become the best person they can be, and the other does the same.

Right relationships feel like an elevator ride up that will never end! The more you love yourself in those relationships, the more you can love them, and vice-versa. These are the pairings we should seek and cherish, for many of us have another type of love—one that resembles a seesaw. It's an unbalanced selfish love where partners beg for sacrifices and compromises. We love ourselves less and less so they can feel better about themselves. There is no ascending together for the better. Avoid egocentric, insecure people who aren't concerned about your upward elevation.

Remember, you're no stepping stone for someone else.

Posting

"The moment you post your relationship on Facebook, things get messy and problems arise. I'd rather keep my relationship a secret."

That's what we tell ourselves, but that isn't really the truth. Facebook is just an app used by your so-called friends. If posting about your relationship on social media makes things messy, it's probably because you have messy so-called friends. They're "so-called" because we don't know most of them personally. So I ask you, why do you give them so much control? If you feel reserved about sharing that you're in a relationship, it might be time to filter your friends list and audit your inner circle.

Of course, I'm not saying post all your business on Facebook, I'm suggesting that you care more about what your partner thinks. Make the appropriate steps to enjoy your relationship without restriction.

Remember, as painful as it is to admit, proper social media etiquette is vital to modern relationships.

Forgiveness Bank

People don't build up enough equity in their second chances and forgiveness bank to earn that second chance. Then when they want it, they're confused when you don't give it to them. They didn't see the value in doing the little things until it was too late.

In the little things, people can show that being faithful, compassionate, considerate, and trustworthy is a part of who they are. And they can show that being sheisty, deceptive, and untruthful is not.

Those little things provide us with an opportunity to evaluate character one small gesture at a time. When a positive action is displayed in even the smallest situation, a deposit is made into that second chances bank.

So use that person's account balance to decide if what they did to offend us was a mistake or a predictable event—not undue sympathy or unchecked emotions.

It's not your fault he didn't value the little things and use them to prove to you that he wasn't that mistake he just made. So don't fault yourself for having to move on.

Remember, check that forgiveness bank account balance before you offer forgiveness.

Direct Questions

If I ask you a direct question, I expect a direct response.

Do you love me? The response I want is yes or no.

Not blinking or stuttering. Not answering my direct question with a question.

Direct questions deserve direct responses.

Direct Question: "Hey, did you cheat on me?"

Not-So-Direct Response: "Uh, what? I mean, why would you think that? Why would you think I cheated on you?"

If you ask a direct question and get an indirect response, that's cause to be suspicious.

Entertaining Not-So-Direct Responses breed distrust, give way to confusion and cause reason for doubt. Expect people to be clear, direct and truthful with you. No tricks, no gimmicks—yes, they love you, or no, they don't.

Uncertainty Words

We need to stop falling for uncertainty words. When people say, "You know, I could see us possibly being together in the future. If we ever live that long. If, you know, things are going good. If it continues at the same rate...multiplied by two divided by pi...add the square root of whatever...Yeah, I can see us working out if you continue to grow and get ready and push past the heartbreak. I mean, I'm ready for a relationship, but that's if I ever make sense of things in my life."

Come on. If somebody wants be with you, there will be no uncertainty in their words. They're going to say, "I want to be with you." It isn't difficult. It isn't complicated.

Remember, when somebody loves you, they will say, "I love you." without if's, might's or maybe's.

Lie Is the Reason

I hate it when a cheater lies about their indiscretion; as if lying wasn't the reason they're in that position in the first place.

You think you're protecting me with those lies? When you get busted, you say, "I wanted to protect you, I didn't want to hurt you." You hurt me when you slept with that person.

Listen, your lying is the problem. Your lying is the reason you cheated. You think you just lied after you cheated? No, you were lying well before.

If you were honest and had told the truth from the beginning, we could've prevented this.

If you'd told the truth about meeting that person you shouldn't have been talking to, we could've prevented this.

If you'd told the truth about where you were going and whom you were with, we could've prevented this.

If you'd told the truth about me and how you were feeling in this relationship, maybe I could've helped.

If you'd told the truth about me not bringing that "spice" you needed in this relationship, maybe I could've changed.

But you didn't. You lied from the beginning, and now you think continuing those lies is going to help. Maybe you should start telling the truth. That's the only way I can help you.

Remember, cheating is the result of many betrayals, lies, and mistakes. The deception started well before the deed was done.

Afraid of Honesty

Too many people are afraid of honesty. They're afraid of what honesty may do to their relationship. Their truth may lead to their partner behaving in a certain way—or even leaving. Understand that working out a problem in a relationship sometimes means going your separate ways.

But still, you worked the problem out. You eliminated that thorn in your flesh. Yes, you hope you can simply extract the thorn from the rose, but sometimes, you have to get rid of the rose completely.

Either way, you start to heal. You start to grow. You start to be able to feel again. You have to work it out, but you can't do that if you're not being honest about your feelings. Always be truthful, so either way, you can grow to love yourself.

Remember, working it out doesn't always mean staying.

Problems

You have to fully commit. There is no other option in relationships when problems arise. You should either be all the way invested or checked out completely. Both choices resolve the present issue.

Here's what people do instead—they don't choose one path. They waffle, go back and forth, keep one foot in and one foot out. Half-assing a solution oftentimes breeds more complications and difficulties because no one direction was given the attention and effort it needed to be successful. It takes one hundred percent of ourselves to fix a destructive relationship pattern—or to leave the relationship altogether.

If you're in this type of dilemma, realize it's okay to step back and take some time to figure out what you want and how you want to achieve it. Once you decide you want to fix or abandon it, stick with the decision.

Remember, you'll only be successful at something when you're completely invested in it. That includes relationships.

Needs Are the Reason You Cheated

I hate it when people say, "I've got needs. That's the reason I cheated."

I've got needs, too, but they haven't ever made me cheat. You know what my needs are?

I need somebody loyal. I need somebody faithful. I need somebody with integrity. I need somebody who can be my partner, a companion. I need somebody who can show me love. I need somebody who can communicate.

I've got needs, too, but none of those needs make me step out on anybody. If meeting your needs means you're going to step out on me, then step out of my life.

You need to get a life. You need to get a clue. You need to grow up because you're being childish. If your need to cheat trumps my need to be with a good person, then you don't need to be in a relationship with me. You need to be by yourself. You need a Netflix password and a dog. You don't need a relationship.

Remember, no need is ever worth cheating to meet.

Love and Leave

Just because I love you doesn't mean I don't have the power to leave you if you do something stupid, disrespect me, or don't treat me the way I deserve to be treated. Don't think for one second that my love doesn't mean I can't love you far away from your arms where you can't hurt me anymore. No, I don't have to hate you to leave you. I just have to know you aren't the right person for me.

Are you doing what's necessary to prove you're worthy of my love, just like I'm agreeing to do for you? Or are you thinking that love is just enough?

I realized in second grade that I needed more than love. Someday, I would need somebody who could communicate, who was kind and patient. Are you willing to be that person for me? If not, then my love for you isn't permission to tolerate what I don't deserve. Because I can love you from far away. I don't have to be right here to love you. I can bounce if you don't treat me right. And I will.

Remember, love is never enough.

Think vs. Know

You know it isn't working. You know the man is cheating on you. She's hitting you. She's disrespecting you. You are disrespecting him. There is too much going on between you.

Yet what do you tell your friends? "Man, I think...I mean...I think I might have to leave. Maybe."

You think? Might? Maybe? No, you have to.

Some people are too unsure to make a decision. So they stay until they finally get the courage. By that point, the damage has been done.

"Oh, I have to leave. NOW."

Don't be that person. Quit waiting. Quit wondering. Quit pondering. You know it and you feel it, so use that knowledge to make a decision. Maybe the reason you're unhappy is that you can't make a decision—leave or stay. Maybe you keep making excuses to keep yourself from acting on what you know in your heart.

Remember, most people only say, "I think it's not going to work," after they realize that it won't.

Being

Relationships shouldn't be measured in hard times, but hard times endured should count for something. When coupled with hitting milestones and achieving successes, enduring the rough patches is a quality you don't want to overlook.

It's not easy being in someone's corner all the time. You undoubtedly have some issues and faults that affect the relationship. Mistakes have been made on your part, but that person is still there, being.

One of the qualities on my mate list is their ability to just be there. Can they be there during the times of trial and seasons of trouble? Will they be there if and when sickness plagues and doubt creeps? Will they be there just to be there for no other reason than being there?

Yes, just being there, just getting through tough times should never be the most important factor in the journey of a relationship. Love should be first, but endurance is not far behind.

Remember, anyone can love you when it's easy and the path is clear, so search for the one who can also be there for you when it isn't.

Placeholding

Some people see their relationships as placeholders for better opportunities. That's it. Sometimes, the person you thought loved you really didn't love you, they just loved you placeholding for someone better to come along. Then they leave you in shambles.

Or you leave them in shambles. Sometimes, we're the guilty ones. We sit in the relationship even though we know it isn't going to work out. We're not where we need to be emotionally, so we stay in the relationship until we get our self-confidence back up, until we find somebody who appreciates us. Maybe we wait until we graduate college, get that new job, or the kids are old enough to move out.

But let me tell you something—it's dangerous to placehold for so long. When it's time to let go, you can't because you've been holding on so long. You don't know what else to do.

Remember, stop staying in relationships for the wrong reasons. Stop placeholding.

Walk Away

There's a man at the end of the aisle waiting for you. He's standing next to your father. He's standing next to his best man, and your best friend is watching.

They're all watching you walk down that aisle in your white dress looking radiant. Your man is waiting for you to walk toward him.

But you ain't there yet. You know why? Because you haven't walked away from that problem. You haven't walked away from that hindrance. You haven't walked away from that pain. You haven't walked away from that heartbreak.

To walk toward your future and your future husband, to walk down that aisle toward your father, your best friend, and his best man, you have to walk away from that person. You know who I mean. That person who keeps you away from your happiness.

Life is very simple. There are two different types of walks in life. There is that walk away, and that walk toward. Are you afraid to walk away? Is that the reason you can't walk toward your sunshine? Only you know. But what I do know is this—a man is waiting at the end of the aisle for you. Will you meet him there? Or are you too afraid?

Remember, you can either walk toward your future and walk away from your past, or you can walk toward your past and walk away from you future.

Okay Love

Standing in the way of most extraordinary loves are mountains built from the overflow of average ones. If great relationships were heroes, average ones would most certainly be the villains. No, they're not abusive, unfaithful or controlling, but okay relationships have long been extraordinary relationships' greatest enemy.

Average relationships have the ability to sorta work for us. They fulfill some wants and needs we ask for, and there is minimal heartache and little friction, which makes them hard to leave. You may know that it's not what you really want, but there is never an inexcusable act or wrongdoing that provides an obvious reason to break up. All the while, the hero of your love story never meets you because a just okay guy did first.

Think about the relationship you're in or consider building. Is it what you want, or do you feel like you're settling? That feeling of settling is the biggest tell of an average relationship.

Remember, never settle. Never settle. Never settle.

Sixty Days

Are you too afraid to endure the sixty days filled with the heartache, heartbreak, stress, second-guessing, and lonely nights that come from leaving a negative relationship?

It is that fear that often leads us to forfeit the next sixty years of potential happiness with the right person. At times, we allow the prospect of a difficult next sixty days post break up to break up the very promising future we have waiting for us once we leave. Yes, breaking it off with that person isn't going to be easy, nor should it be. But it is necessary. It won't be without pain, tears, and brief periods of regret. But we can't let that paralyze us from the sixty years after that's sure to revive us. When you grew older and have lived the rest of your life with the right person, the pain you had to endure from leaving the wrong person will be merely a footnote in your success story.

Remember, sixty years of happiness is worth the sixty days of discomfort it takes to achieve it.

When things are falling apart and you don't know what to do, don't be afraid to leave. Don't shut up that voice in the back of your head. Don't let somebody else make you live life the way they think you should. Nobody else can walk the path to your sunshine but you. And sometimes, you have to walk that path alone.

Leave that negative relationship.

Recover

In a negative relationship? It's possible to recover.

Love Has Your Back

Love has always had your back. It hasn't ever left you. You just have to turn around and see it. Maybe you're too afraid to do so. Maybe you're too connected to the wrong person who isn't supposed to be in your life, and you don't want to turn your back on them.

But to get to your happiness, you have to! You have to turn your back on hurtful people, negative thoughts, and that unhealthy amount of guilt. Then walk away. Walk toward a future beyond that person and that life you don't want.

Believe me, there is love at the end of the aisle waiting, ready to marry you. But you will never see it if you refuse to turn from the guy who isn't the one. Love has always been standing there, waiting for you. Yes, in the search of finding it, you'll have to turn your back on people and walk away.

Remember, your happiness is worth those steps to turn around.

Heartbreak

Everybody on earth has experienced some type of heartbreak. It touches everyone, even that girl on your Instagram feed who's saying, "I said yes! I said yes! Yes!" Even she's experienced heartbreak before. The only difference is, she decided not to allow it to define her. She decided to let it go.

I know people who say, "Yo, it's so hard to let go. It's too hard." No, it's not. Physically letting go is one action that takes five fingers. But mentally letting go is different. Sometimes, we talk ourselves out of decisions we need to make. Sometimes, we put barriers in front of our own heads. Sometimes, we don't dismiss thoughts that keep us around negative people and negative experiences.

You need to decide first—are you going to let go or not? Then, let go so you can find your own "I said yes" moment.

Remember, you can't catch your Mr. Right while holding on to Mr. Wrong.

Cleanse Your Palate

Far too often, we can't enjoy the juice of a great life someone has to offer us because our taste buds are tainted by the past. Despite those negative people, experiences, and times in your life, are you willing to cleanse your pallet? Are you willing to put that ginger on your tongue so you can fully taste the fruits of your destiny?

Or are you letting your taste buds be held captive by the pain? The mistrust? The negative experience with that person who didn't belong in your life in the first place?

Life isn't as sweet when we refuse to wash away decayed thoughts that continue to interfere in our attempts to enjoy it. So cleanse your palate so you can taste what life has to give you fully without the bitterness.

Remember, love is sweet. Are you willing to taste it?

Your Soulmate?

Who told you that person was your soulmate?

Did God come down and say, "Hey, that's the person I made for you"?

I'm telling you, unless God himself came down and told you that one specific person is your soulmate and will always be your soulmate, I don't believe you.

"They're my twin flame! We're destined to be together! We'll stand the test of time!"

Really? You don't know that! Quit anointing people as soulmates too early. You're too afraid to leave that person who isn't good for you because you confuse soulmate with heartmate. Some people are good for your heart, not your soul. Who can know your heart? It's the most treacherous thing you have.

So don't confuse your soulmate with your heartmate, your bodymate, or your fakemate. Some people out there will pretend to look like a real soulmate, but they're not.

Remember, only time will tell who your soulmate really is, not lust.

8:01

If we break up at 8:00 p.m., I'm absolutely clueless about what's going on in your life at 8:01. When we break up, I cut things off—everything. People are going to ask me if I saw your post on the 'gram. I didn't because I blocked you.

Does that make me petty? Yes, I'm petty, but I'm also protecting my sanity. I don't want to physically meet up with my ex in person, so why would I meet up with that person mentally by texting, talking, and scrolling?

I have to break up with that person mentally, too. So at 8:01 and after, I'm not in a space where I can start to care. If I were, I'd get jealous. I'd regret the breakup. I might even think about getting back into the relationship, which isn't good for me. I have to protect my heart. Sometimes, that means I have to be petty and block somebody.

I am going to throw the idea of you so far away from my environment that there is no possibility I can allow you to pop up in my mind and tempt me to re-engage you.

So at 8:01 after you break up with me or I break up with you, you will be blocked. Sorry, it may seem petty, but it's a step I must take to get over you and begin to heal my heart.

Remember, petty people are also sane people.

Don't Subtract

If you find somebody who's goal-oriented, already happy, who "has it all together," know that one of the most important adages to their life is their ability to not subtract from it.

For those individuals who are already assembled before we meet them, there is no need for building. Just focus on not tearing them apart!

Don't come into their lives until you're sure you won't sabotage what they have going on and bring drama to an otherwise peaceful life.

Have you noticed sadness only arrives after we get into the wrong relationship? Yes, the goal may be to find someone who is ready for a successful pairing, but what if you're not? We have to be responsible enough not to disrupt the joy of others while searching for ours.

Simply put, add. Add. Add. Don't take away.

Remember, just avoid fucking up a happy life.

Finger Button

People try to solve their problems the wrong way. Right now, you've got a problem with an ex-boyfriend or a boyfriend's girlfriend or a side piece. You want to tell them about themselves. You want to say, "Hey, I want to talk to you. So I can tell you how much I don't want you in my life no more. So I can tell you to stop talking to me and stop trying to text me."

Every time you try to move on them and pop in their inbox, all you need is a finger and a button.

All this time, you've been trying to figure out a fancy way to tell that person you don't want to talk to them anymore. What you need is a finger and button.

Finger.

Button.

I'm talking about the block button! Yet you still want to spend more time talking, figuring shit out, and wasting valuable time you could use to grow you, be there for you, and move on to your own life goals.

Remember, quit wasting time on people who don't deserve yours. All you need is a finger and a block button.

Give-a-Fuck Budget

I'm on a give-fuck-budget. I've been struggling with my give-a-fucks. After I pay everybody off, I don't have much remaining. I have to give a fuck about people I actually give a fuck about—my parents and friends, the people who want to be in my life, the people who treat me well and appreciate me.

I give a fuck about them. But after that, I only have a few left over. I would give you one, but when you had my love, you didn't appreciate me. You should've taken advantage of the fuck I gave you. But you didn't. And now you want to talk after we're broken up? Now you want me to give a fuck? I don't carry spare fucks in my pocket. I only have credit, and I won't be swiping it on you ever again.

Remember, nobody deserves all of your fucks. You're on a limited budget.

It takes Heart

Just because I shut you out doesn't mean I don't love you. As a matter of fact, it is the very proof that I do. It pains me to see you struggle after this break-up, and as much as it hurts me to stand by and watch you attempt to reach out to me, I cannot be the person to help you through this. Together, we are the source of the pain that both you and I are experiencing. It's unhealthy for both of us. You may think I'm cold and heartless for taking this stance, but you don't know how many times I thought about unblocking you...how many times I started to text you, then deleted it...how many times I dialed your number, even though your name's not saved in my phone.

You don't understand how close I was to giving in—because I care about you. But that would be destructive for our growth apart. Think about it, how would you grow if I acted like nothing happened? Like everything is good after you treated me like shit? How would I heal?

Shutting you out takes discipline. Understand how easy it would've been for me to keep talking to you and continue the cycle. But we both know that's not for the best.

Remember, breaking an unhealthy relationship cycle doesn't make you heartless. It's actually evidence that you have one.

We Isn't We

When my pronouns change, so does my attitude. When we were together, there were a lot of we's, us's, and let's because my life included you. We were a team, and I'm a great team player. We won and lost together. I remember saying, "What are we going to eat? What are we going to do? Where are we going to live?"

But you're no longer in my life. There is no more we, it's simply me. My pronouns changed, so my attitude must as well. I have to worry about me, not you, not us. The "you" word is none of my business anymore. You are no longer someone I am concerned about.

So if we are we, value and cherish that. If you show that "us" is actually "you," then I have to just be about me—and I really do that well.

Remember, we is always we—not you.

Capable

"I've been working on myself. I've been getting myself together. I thought about all the things you said when we broke up. I'm saying to myself, 'Damn. I really need to change.' I realize how much I hurt you. I'm a different person. We should work this out."

Have you heard something like that before? If so, listen—I don't doubt that they may have changed somewhat. Maybe all those words are completely true, but I'm not concerned about that. I want you to think long and hard about what that person is capable of instead!

After that person hurt you, did their DNA change? Do they still look exactly like they did when they disrespected you? I bet they have the same name and sound just as they did before, don't they? Maybe they've changed, but they're the same person who is capable of the same things. So consider who that person was—and is—before allowing them to rejoin your life.

Remember, fool you once, shame on them. Fool you twice, your heart gets broken all over again.

Representative

The only reason we give people a second chance is that we're still in love with the person they *were*, not with who the person is *now*. We have to be able to tell the difference.

Look, you fell in love with that person's representative. They sent their job interview self. They answered some questions correctly and told you what you wanted to hear. For that probation period, they watched their P's and Q's. They showed up for the relationship job on time and did what they were supposed to do. But once you gave them the full-time benefits, they relaxed into the person they were before they met you.

You miss that person, the person you hired to be your boyfriend or girlfriend. But guess what—they never really were that person. Your relationship never really worked with that person's true self. So quit missing that person. They were never that person to begin with. They were always the person who fooled you.

Remember, if that person changes on you once you start dating, chances are, they never were the person you thought they were.

From Over There

You're still having problems with ex-boyfriends because you need distance between yourself and them. Distance. Every time you let that person back into your life, they start bringing headaches, problems, and pain you don't want.

"What you need to do is be his friend," people will say. Sure. Maybe. Maybe you can be his friend. But if you're going to be his friend, you have to be his friend from over there—way over there.

"We're cool. Don't get me wrong, we're cool. Just from over there. If I see you in public, I'm going to say hello. But I'm going to have to yell because I'm going to be standing over there. I'm going to be over there because I don't want you to bring your problems near me. Maybe we can be friends, yes. But if so, it will have to be far way over there."

Remember, you can still be friends—from over there.

Lonely in a Relationship

I'd rather pay for Netflix every month for the rest of my life, feed ten cats, have to delete my internet history, and sanitize my computer every night for the rest of my life than stay with somebody who doesn't appreciate me. I am not afraid to be alone.

I can deal with the prospect of growing old and being alone. It's being lonely with somebody who doesn't love me that terrifies me the most. To spend the rest of my life watching someone slowly become unrecognizable is a fate I will not accept.

People will try to use their companionship against you. They will assume that you're too used to this relationship to be single again. Remind them that you will take alone over loneliness with them every time. Expect them never to isolate you in the household you two share.

Remember, touch your chest daily as a reminder of the only constant thing that's guaranteed to be in your life—you.

Leech

Have you ever noticed that you felt good about yourself *before* you got into a relationship? Your self-esteem is high, you're confident, and you're filled with so many smiles. But soon afterwards, you start to feel drained, emotionally fatigued, and those smiles fade. This happens when we don't protect ourselves from leeches in soulmate's clothing. It starts slowly at first. One small compromise at a time, and you barely notice them sucking away your happiness. By the relationship's end, your self-worth is depleted and your heart is out of resources. They steal our resources to improve their lives. Then they leave the relationship in good spirits, revitalized and ready to date another.

You have to recognize the signs. Leeches only take. They provide little in exchange for the benefits you provide them. Often they'll boast about their potential and love one-sided partnerships. Try to only enter relationships that are equally beneficial, where both people can build.

Remember, never break yourself trying to fix someone else.

Where Was This?

It seems like people want to get themselves together once we're broken up.

"Hold on! Where was this person when we were dating? Now you have your goals together, now you have your life straight, now you're doing all those things I asked you to do for me? Now you're doing it for that person?"

Look, some people aren't compatible with us. It's a hard fact. A great guy for that girl may not be a great guy for you, and vice-versa. Compatibility is key. It's not that the person changed once they got out of the relationship. It's just that now, they've found the right person to make them the best them they can be.

And you need to focus on who can make you the best you can be, too. Obviously, it wasn't that person. So quit worrying about what they're doing, what they have going on, and how much they've improved. Rather, focus more on finding and improving you. Your energy is better served there.

Remember, find the person you can make a better *them*, who can also make you a better *you*.

Need vs. Want

We have to learn to be attracted to what we need and not just what we want. Some neglect this vital step by dismissing their pattern of finding bad potential mates to a shallow dating pool, bad luck, or the "only attracting the wrong men" theory.

Here's the thing—we don't only attract the wrong type of attention. You're awesome, and all types of men are drawn to that. It's more about the ones who already fancy us that we choose to entertain. Consider that there may be a defect in the process of how we pick partners.

Is it possible you are only allured by qualities in the opposite sex that are not exactly what you need, but what you want?

We need to go back to the drawing board, recondition our desires, and discipline ourselves to value needs above wants in all cases. We need not allow things that fade with time like appearance to be more important than a good heart.

You are not a bad guy magnet, you just need to learn how to repel what you don't need just because it's something you want.

Remember, needs are the attributes we cannot live without in a relationship. Wants are the sugar on top.

Prove Them Wrong

The biggest slap-in-the-face moment we experience after a breakup is when people who warned us about the person who mistreated us say, "I told you so."

It's a bitter feeling. You have to come to terms with what you did. You sided with your heart instead of the sound reasoning and concerns of your friends.

But what's even worse than *hearing* that old adage is *being* the person those words are about. You told people how awesome you were, and you proved them wrong. You have no defense if you can't be everything you claim to be.

Remember, that person will have to answer to their love ones after a heart break. The story doesn't end at your wrongdoing.

List for YOU

What good is it to find a perfect mate for yourself—someone who causes you to cross everything off the wish list for a good husband or a good wife—if you haven't also crossed things off their list, too?

Relationships fail because people put too much energy into other people. Right now, you're single. You focus so much on whether this or that person is a good man or woman for you. But you ignore the fact that maybe you have to be a good man or woman, too. What qualities do you want to have as a wife or husband?

Write those down right now. Quit worrying about other people reaching those standards. Be disciplined enough to stay out of a relationship until you become what you think a good spouse should be.

Remember, it's no good to find the perfect person for you if you're not the perfect person for them.

Sorry

I only have a few sorry's in my tank. I can say, "Sorry," only so many times, especially after I've done everything I can to make this right. Yes, I know I hurt you. I know I caused you pain. I made myself available to do whatever I could to atone, to earn your forgiveness.

But I can't make you forgive me. You have to choose to. Even if you don't, I'm not going to live in misery just because you didn't offer forgiveness or a second chance. I'm not going to sulk, be unhappy, or not move on with my life. No, I'm going to better myself and change. Just because you don't forgive me doesn't mean I shouldn't forgive myself.

You see me in pictures smiling, moving on, and being happy with other people. Because I am. No, I'm not the same person that hurt you. I've changed—even if you don't believe so or you refuse to see for yourself.

Remember, give yourself a second chance before asking others to give you one.

Closure

Just because another person refuses to work with you to close a dark chapter in the life you two shared, you're going to let them hold your recovery hostage? You don't need that person for closure! Yes, finding atonement is easier when someone openly forgives us and helps us feel less shitty about the mistakes we made, but that's not always an option. Regardless, you have to close that door so you're not consistently haunted by demons hiding in that past. You can do it! You've closed doors all your life by yourself. All you ever needed were five fingers and the palm of your own hand.

Remember, closure will always be your responsibility to find, for it is you who suffers without it.

Walk into Your Sunshine

Nobody said it was going to be easy. Nobody said you wouldn't stay up all night crying. Nobody said your heart wouldn't feel like it was breaking in half. Nobody said you weren't going to lose weight, that you weren't going to be stressed out, that you weren't going to wonder whether you made the right decision or not. Nobody said you wouldn't have to deal with those demons after leaving the negative relationship behind. Nobody said you weren't going to care for that person, that you wouldn't like that person any more, that your love for that person would disappear right away.

Sometimes, people can abuse us and mistreat us, but we still care because we're good people. But you have to stay on the path out of that relationship, no matter how difficult it feels or how much it hurts. Eventually, you're going to walk into your sunshine. The pain will have been worth it. But you have to keep walking.

Remember, your sunshine is out there. So keep walking.

Love What Makes Me, Me

How can you love me but not love the things that make me, *me*? I didn't just magically appear out of nowhere, a man without a past. That past shaped the person you love. Yet you're now trying to make me feel ashamed of my experiences. That will not happen! I embrace all of them—the mistakes, the heartbreaks, the successes. Without those experiences, there would be no me and no us.

To complete your healing, accept the role your past played in making you the beautiful being you are today. The journey is already difficult enough, too difficult to willingly add another set of judging eyes inside your circle of trust to make you feel bad for who you used to be. That's not love.

Remember, everyone has a past. Some people focus on the skeletons in your closet to avoid dealing with the graveyard in theirs.

What about You

You want what's best for everybody else. Every time you turn around, you're putting somebody else's needs in front of yours. That's your nurturing nature. I understand you have to make sure everybody around you is doing good, but what about you? How are you doing? You're asking about everybody else's day, but how is yours? You listen to everybody's problems, but do you listen to yours?

It's okay to put yourself first. It's okay to treat yourself. And it's okay to not feel guilty about it either. Just because you're doing things for yourself doesn't mean other people have to go without. Your responsibility is to make sure you're okay. You can't make sure everybody else is okay while you're suffering. You can't make sure everybody else is happy if you're unhappy. It's okay to take care of yourself and treat yourself right.

Remember, your needs come first.

Not to Heal

The time between relationships should be the time to have a relationship with yourself. Too many people skip this crucial step. They busy themselves with rebound relationships to mask the pain instead of using that time to heal and love themselves again.

Going from breakup to rebound without a season of self-love starts a never-ending cycle where you get into another relationship, then another and another. You're never able to find the satisfaction you desire because no other person can ever fill that void of self-love.

Be as eager to find a relationship with yourself as you are with another person. Maybe if you do that first, the other one will work.

Remember, no one can love you the way you love yourself.

It's Your Job

Just as it's your job to make sure you're happy, it's also your job to ensure that no one makes you unhappy. Those are both vital tasks that you and you alone are responsible for—yet they're often overlooked.

Some will say, "He makes me so unhappy," displacing responsibility and blame, distracting us from the real culprit: us. Yes, it's a tough truth to swallow. But at best, people can only influence our emotions, never control them. Stop getting so wrapped up in holding others accountable for your misery that you ignore the most powerful tool you possess—choice. You can choose not to allow anyone to chip away your joy!

Remember, it is not enough to find happiness, you must also protect it.

Not Stressed

Look at you looking all scrumptious, looking like you aren't stressed out by anyone causing you problems. Look at you wearing your stress-free, walking away like you spent all night loving yourself, not starving yourself.

Why do you look that way? Because you haven't spent all night arguing with somebody. You don't have bags under your eyes because you're in a healthy relationship with yourself. You're not losing weight. You're not wrinkled. You're not having problems. You're not having anxiety. You love yourself. You're not letting somebody wear you down. Look at you right now, looking like you got rid of the problem that caused your health problems.

When you're with the wrong person, you wear them and their problems. You wear them on your skin and hold them in your bones. I can tell.

But you got rid of that problem. You're smiling again. You're loving yourself again. You're looking and feeling young again.

Remember, people can tell when you're with the wrong person. So don't be.

Smile Regardless

I'm going to smile when I meet you. I'm going to smile on our first date. I'm going to smile when we fall in love. I'm going to smile when we pick out a house together.

I'm going to smile after you decide to break my heart. I'm going to smile when I start taking steps forward again. I'm going to smile when I'm fighting with myself again. I'm going to smile when I realize that nobody in life is going to break me. I'm going to smile when I meet the person who is supposed to be in my life—and it isn't you.

I'm going to smile when that person treats me right, is truthful with me, and does everything they say they're going to. I'm going to smile when I appreciate myself for my resiliency, knowing there isn't anyone who can stop my smiles.

Remember, I will always smile.

It's not too late. It's not too late for that relationship. It's not too late for love. Love can still be everything you imagined it can be. But recovery takes both of you—both of you all in all the time.

In a negative relationship? It's possible to recover.

ABOUT ACE METAPHOR

This book was inspired by you, for you.
I am merely the vessel, the voice.
Therefore –
This book is not about me.
But rather,
About you.
www.acemetaphor.com

Made in the USA
Monee, IL
16 August 2020

38582844R00069